Watercolor Impressions

Pat Maixner Magaret & Donna Ingram Slusser

That Patchwork Place®

Credits

Technical Editor .... Kerry Hoffman
Managing Editor .... Greg Sharp
Copy Editor .... Tina Cook
Proofreader .... Leslie Phillips
Design Director .... Judy Petry
Cover & Text Designer .... David Chrisman
Production Assistant .... Shean Bemis
Photographer .... Brent Kane
Photography Assistant .... Richard Lipshay

Watercolor Impressions

© 1995 by Pat Maixner Magaret and Donna Ingram Slusser
That Patchwork Place, Inc., PO Box 118
Bothell, WA 98041-0118 USA

Printed in Hong Kong
00 99 98   6 5 4

Mission Statement

We are dedicated to providing quality products that
encourage creativity and promote self-esteem
in our customers and our employees.

We strive to make a difference in the lives we touch.

*That Patchwork Place is an employee owned,
financially secure company.*

Library of Congress Cataloging-in-Publication Data
Magaret, Pat Maixner,
    Watercolor impressions / Pat Maixner Magaret and Donna Ingram Slusser.
       p.   cm.
    ISBN 1-56477-116-4
    1. Patchwork quilts. 2. Color in textile crafts. I. Slusser, Donna Ingram. II. Title.
    TT835.M337 1995
    746.46–dc20   95-32933
                                                               CIP

CONTENTS

Beyond *Watercolor Quilts* (Our First Book) 4

From Our Mailbox 6

Work Spaces and Design Inspirations 8

What's New in Visual Surface Texture 10

   Smoothy Fabrics 10

   Chunky Fabrics 11

   Transition Fabrics 13

   Creating Flowers 15

   Sorting by Visual Texture 19

Creative Expression—You Can Do It 20

   Myths About Creativity 22

   Sources of Inspiration 27

   Work or Play? 29

   Planning a Specific Design 31

   Where Do I Go from Here? 35

Gallery 36

Afterword—Thanks and Good Luck! 110

   Bibliography 111

Our grateful appreciation to:

   The staff at That Patchwork Place, Inc., for their guidance and encouragement, which is always given cheerfully and graciously;

   The quiltmakers whose creative efforts and thoughts appear in this book;

   Kumamoto, Japan, International Exchange Section, for permission to use their quilt "A River Runs Through It";

   South Sea Imports and Katie Frym, for contributing fabrics to this project and for giving us the opportunity to develop our inspirations into fabric designs;

   Hoffman California Fabrics, and P & B Textiles, for contributing fabrics;

   Cheryl Greenstreet Swain of Country Stitches, Genessee, Idaho, for her beautiful machine quilting when Pat ran out of time for hand quilting;

   Our Earth for nature's abundant inspiration;

   Pat's family (David, Craig, Nate, and Anna);

   Donna's family (Lloyd, Alan, Kirstin, Larry, and Nicole), who have come to appreciate late-hour meals, stacks of 2" squares on furniture, and weeds in the garden. Their encouragement has always been steadfast and sincere.

Special thanks to:

   Anna and Lloyd, for cutting 2" squares when our supply ran low.
   Abby, Lily, and Muffin, for helping us keep on track.

BEYOND *WATERCOLOR QUILTS*
(OUR FIRST BOOK)

*T*wo years ago we wrote *Watercolor Quilts*, which features Impressionistic scrap quilts made from 2" squares of multicolored fabrics. The watercolor technique is named for its similarity to watercolor painting. The fabrics in quilts made with this technique gradually move from dark to light, like a watercolor wash, and colors shift smoothly from one to another.

The forerunner of the watercolor quilt is the Colourwash series made by English quilt artist and author Deirdre Amsden. We noticed that Deirdre's Impressionistic style of using small shapes to blend and shade colors across the surface of quilts was similar to value studies we had made. Our watercolor quilts went in a different direction from Deirdre Amsden's. We developed representational and pictorial design themes, incorporated traditional

block designs, used appliqué, and re-created blossoms in our work.

Since the publication of *Watercolor Quilts* we have seen an explosion of excitement about this type of scrap quilt. New quilters are attracted to the watercolor style because of the ease of construction. Many longtime quiltmakers, who have successfully mastered basic sewing and quilting techniques, are looking for a new way to express their ideas and want to concentrate on the design process.

Whatever their experience level, quiltmakers around the world agree—making watercolor quilts is addictive. Once you get started you just can't stop moving those little squares around on the design wall. As with a jigsaw puzzle, you become obsessed with the search for the "perfect piece."

We wrote this book as a way of celebrating and thanking all quiltmakers who are hooked on watercolor techniques. *Watercolor Impressions* also gives us the opportunity to share more beautiful quilts.

To those who ask: Where do ideas come from? How do I take my idea and run with it? How can I get those same beautiful results? How can I become an artist? Stay tuned! We hope you find inspiration on every page.

He who works with his hands is a laborer:
He who works with his head and his hands is
a craftsman:
He who works with his head and his hands and
his heart is an artist.

Author Unknown

FROM OUR MAILBOX

We just love all the mail we receive—through the U.S. Postal System, on-line computer services, and electronic mail. We even get messages on our telephone answering machines. Mail comes to us from around the world, from students who have been in our classes and from quilters we have never met. We see photographs of quilts in progress and photographs of finished quilts. We delight in our mail and are happy to share some of these quiltmakers' thoughts with you.

Terry Waldron wrote, "I would carry my design into different parts of the house. While I was cooking or even grading papers, I wanted to be able to sneak a peek now and then to make sure the fabric squares blended properly. One night, I knew I'd passed into 'the outer limits' when I set my design wall against the banister outside our bedroom so that I could see my design as soon as I woke up."

Sandy Boyd wrote, "I design around a particular fabric or family of colors or prints and let them tell me what they need. After a while, the groups of prints in watercolor quilts have voices of their own and become quite bossy. The whole process can be engrossing. One of my students suggested we start a Watercolor Support Group because we were becoming compulsive!"

Watercolor quilts even go on vacation. After returning from a trip to Italy, Julia Rosekrans wrote, "We took 1½" squares of fabric with us, intending to do a watercolor project, but we were so busy sightseeing that the only time left for playing with fabric was on a long bus ride from Florence to Sorrento.

We taped interfacing to the bus windows and attached our squares with straight pins." Julia cautions that the one hazard of working on a moving bus is that you can experience a bit of motion sickness!

Helen Matthews sums it all up. "Watercolor quiltmaking is a great dieting tool—you cannot tear yourself away from your design wall. The hours slip by without a thought for anything else, and I keep thinking, 'I'll just move this here and then that there,' but then you can't stop, even for meals."

WORK SPACES AND DESIGN INSPIRATIONS

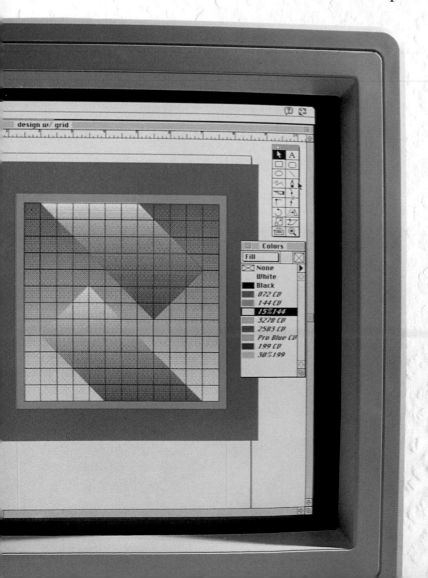

*M*any quiltmakers have been inspired by the projects pictured in *Watercolor Quilts*. Some made quilts based on those in the book, while other quiltmakers used the photographs as inspiration and then added their own twist to the design. In this book, there are three quilts that depict picket fences. It is interesting to see that each artist brought her own background, inspiration, and emotions to the project and expressed herself in a different way.

We have seen watercolor quilts of all sizes. One miniature adaptation featured ½" finished squares. A real treasure! At the opposite end of the scale spectrum, watercolor techniques have been used to make full-size bed quilts. You may ask, What is the best way to design a *large* watercolor quilt? Most design walls are not big enough to accommodate huge quantities of squares. Many of the quiltmakers whose work is featured in this book encountered this problem. Sylvia Richardson commented, "Because I worked with over a thousand squares, I was overwhelmed at times. I solved the problem by working in sections, beginning with the picket fence in the bottom half of the quilt.

After completing the bottom half, I designed the top half." Sylvia's "Spring After the Ice Storm (It Did Come)" is on page 73.

Other quilters have rigged pulley systems at one end of a large room. Their design walls are attached to ropes and can be lowered to the right height as they work on the design. When the room is needed for other purposes, the wall can be raised out of the way. As an alternative, stepladders come in handy when you need to reach the higher areas of your design wall.

It is amazing to hear about the emergence of computers into the quilt world and especially the world of watercolor quilts. There are computer bulletin boards and on-line fabric swaps and exchange groups. "CISter's Sunrise" on page 57 contains many squares from around the world, obtained via a computer watercolor fabric exchange.

More and more, quiltmakers are using their computers to design watercolor quilts. Sherri Vaughn's "Ebb and Flow" on page 91 is an example. She uses her computer rather than graph paper and pencil. Who would ever have guessed that watercolor quilts would be part of the computer age?

Because of watercolor quilts, we can't even get a good night's sleep. We dream about our designs, stay up late, and get up early in order to work on them. Quilters have shown us projects depicting beautiful nighttime landscapes. They confess to staying up through the wee hours of the morning in order to observe the lighting effects of the moon.

We know that no matter what kind of work space you have, how many hours you dedicate to your quiltmaking, or what ideas and emotions you want to convey, watercolor techniques are a great way to express yourself.

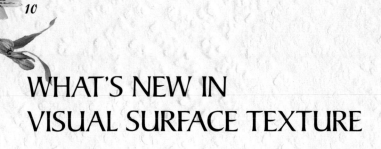

WHAT'S NEW IN VISUAL SURFACE TEXTURE

*A*n *Watercolor Quilts* we briefly discussed color and its properties and gave a summary description of fabric-print design elements, such as scale, line, contrast, and symmetry. Quiltmakers combine these components in many variations to create visual texture.

While teaching watercolor classes, working with students, and making more quilts, the importance of several concepts became evident to us. We now discuss these concepts in detail in our classes. Visual texture is important to the overall design of watercolor quilts. Fabrics used in watercolor quilts should have different colors, contrasting values and intensities, a variety of scales, and asymmetrical lines and designs. We have categorized fabrics into groups. We define these concepts and describe how to use them below.

Smoothy Fabrics

Some fabric prints have an absence of design lines (marks or strokes), which gives them a smooth appearance. Value and color changes in these fabrics are minimal, and most are light in value. We call these fabrics "smoothies."

When smoothy fabric squares are grouped in a design, colors blend, and there are no lines to lead the eye from one square to another. Smooth design areas of light value often create the illusion of a light source emanating from within the quilt or from outside the design. The center of Pat's "Enticement—A Little Peek at Heaven" on page 96 is a good example of how smoothy fabrics can produce a glow that appears to come from within the quilt.

You can create background or open areas with expanses of smoothy

Smoothies

Chunkies

fabrics. Eleanor Cole's "Cathedral on the Rhine" on page 83 demonstrates the effective use of smoothy fabrics to create a backdrop for a design.

Chunky Fabrics

Fabrics that have distinct changes in color and value and that contain strong design lines are what we call "chunkies." Chunky fabrics include all prints that are not smoothies. Groupings of chunky fabrics have more visual texture and a busier appearance than smoothy areas. The design scale of chunky prints ranges from small to large.

Some fabrics have both chunky and smooth patterns. When these fabrics are cut into squares, some squares will contain chunky design elements that reach into the smooth area. Use these squares as "reachies." Use chunky squares with medium- and large-scale flower petals to create blooms in a design.

Group Similar Textures Together

Watercolor designs are most successful when similar textures, values, and colors are placed side by side. If a chunky-textured square is placed in the center of many smoothies, it will stand up and shout, "Help, I don't belong here," or "Hey, look at me. I stand out in a crowd." The same is true if a smoothy-textured square is placed in the middle of a group of chunky-textured squares. Remember, we don't want soloists in our watercolor quilts.

Every square is as important as every other square. Teamwork is the name of the game. It is your job as the quiltmaker to place each player or square in a position that creates harmony.

Above: Notice how a square stands out when its texture is different from that of its neighbors.

Right: All textures, colors, values, and lines blend.

Lines can develop between light and dark areas. Use reachy fabrics and freckle fabrics to make a smooth transition.

Transition Fabrics

When smoothy and chunky areas are placed next to each other in a design, the graded wash effect is lost, and strong lines develop between the contrasting areas. Use reachy fabrics to create a smooth, gradual transition between areas of contrast. Use freckle fabrics to create a *rapid* change between contrasting areas.

Reachy Fabrics

Reachies have a plain or solid-looking background, with lines and colors printed on the fabric that resemble vines, branches, leaves, or flowers extending into space. When these fabrics are cut into squares, they give the subtle appearance of something gently reaching from one area into another. The background value can be light, medium, or dark. (We use those with light values most often, and we use the back side of reachy fabrics for a softer, muted effect.) Watch for these fabrics and start collecting them now.

Use squares of reachy fabrics to lead the eye gradually from a smooth area to a chunky area. Matching values as closely as possible, place a reachy fabric so that

Reachy Fabrics

its darkest side is next to the chunky area of the design and its lightest side is next to the smooth area.

The addition of reachy and freckle fabrics eliminates lines between light and dark areas.

Place reachy squares around the edge of a design element, such as a bouquet, to suggest leaves or delicate baby's breath or ferns. In Doreen Burbank's "A Well-Urned Respite" on page 77, reachies form a feathered edge between the bouquet and the background. Pat Young's "Celestory Window" on page 99 demonstrates how a feathered edge can be used in designs where a garden area meets the sky.

Use reachies to give an impression of hanging or vining flowers. Donna's "Rhapsody in Bloom" on page 36 looks as though wisteria blossoms hang from a pergola in the upper right corner of the quilt.

Freckle Fabrics

Occasionally, the transition between light and dark areas of a design has to be achieved within a short span. It is not always possible to produce a smooth, graded wash effect in a small space. Use "freckle" fabric squares to quickly make a smooth transition between extreme values. Successful freckle fabrics contain both light and dark values and lines and colors that have a fair amount of contrast—what appear to be "freckles." You can find freckle fabrics

with light backgrounds and dark freckles, and others with dark backgrounds and light freckles.

If you want to move from a dark area to a lighter area within your design, place dark-background freckle squares next to the dark area. Then add light-background freckle squares as you get closer to the lighter area. As Pat worked on her "September Spawn" quilt on page 94, she placed dark-background freckle squares next to the solid-appearing dark area. Then she added light-background squares that had dark freckles on them. The addition of a few reachies helped to make a good transition to the smoothy light area.

Freckle Fabrics

Creating Flowers

One of the most frequently asked questions in our workshops is, "How do I create beautiful flowers?" In watercolor quilts, large flowers appear to be made from squares that are all cut from the same floral print. In fact, we make flowers by combining petals or parts of petals from a variety of fabrics.

Watercolor blossoms make use of a "trick-the-eye" technique. When viewed up close, a flower looks like a group of squares with colors and pattern lines that do not match. But when the flower is viewed from a distance, the eye blurs and blends the individual squares. Instead of mismatched fabrics, the viewer sees a pretty, Impressionistic blossom.

Petal Fabrics

Petal Fabrics

It is easy to create flowers when you have a large assortment of "petal" fabric squares that are already sorted. Buy fabrics that have large floral motifs. One fabric often has many different colors and flowers printed on it. In addition, you may find a fabric with several different contrasts—between colors, values, and design lines. When you cut these prints into 2" squares, only parts of the petals, leaves, and other fragmented images remain. They yield an assortment of different petal squares, all from one fabric.

To make it easier to create flowers, sort the petal squares into categories determined by the background value. We have boxes that contain a variety of different-colored petals, all with light backgrounds. We also have boxes of petal squares with medium and dark backgrounds. Within each box, the colors of the background may differ, but their values are the same. Place petals of similar colors next to each other in each box. Don't worry about matching colors exactly.

Petal fabrics sorted by backgrounds—dark, medium, and light groupings

Arrangement of Blossoms

As you create flowers, think of nature. Any single plant has many similar blooms. For example, on a single bush, several roses usually bloom at one time. You can unify segments of a design by repeating a common bloom throughout.

In Pat's "Enticement—A Little Peek At Heaven" on page 96, examine the vining morning glories that appear to hang from the top of her quilt. She found several fabrics with blue vining flowers and used them repeatedly to get the effect she wanted. To add variety and dimension, she added squares cut from other fabrics that contained similar blue vining flowers.

Once you start re-creating flowers it is hard to stop. It is like viewing time-lapse photography in a real flower garden. No need to wait for seeding, pulling weeds, or trimming spent blossoms—you have instant bouquets! The following pointers will help you re-create beautiful flowers in your watercolor quilts.

Re-creating Blossoms

The Background Values Must Be the Same

You can use a variety of background colors in one area, but make sure they are all the same value. For example, in dark areas of your design you can use petals that have black, dark green, and dark red backgrounds. In light areas of your design, use petal squares that have light backgrounds. As long as the background values are the same, the colors don't matter.

Generally, place the darker squares near the bottom of the design and the lighter squares near the top. The darker areas "anchor" the design at the bottom. An example of this effect is found in Pat's "Enticement—A Little Peek At Heaven" on page 96.

Petal Colors Do Not Need to Match

When creating a blossom in your quilt design, the petal values and colors should be similar, but do not need to match exactly. Slight differences in value and color add texture and dimension to flowers, imitating nature. Highlights appear in light portions of the blossom while another portion may be in shadow. Occasionally, adding a petal from a completely different color family adds just the right touch to your flower.

Use Petals Cut from Different Fabrics

For realistic flowers, use petal squares cut from different fabrics or from different flowers in the same fabric. Often, when squares cut from the same flower are placed next to each other, the new blossom looks flat and lacks depth. When you want to create a special effect, or when it is necessary to use several squares that have been cut from the same flower, place the squares kitty-corner from each other. Fill in the remaining squares with similar-colored petals from other fabrics.

Petals cut from same fabric are placed kitty-corner to break up repetition.

Creating the Blossom's Outline

When designing a bloom, it can be helpful to picture the outline of the flower you want to create. The outer edge of the blossom should mimic the gentle curves found in real flowers.

Petals cut from same fabric and placed side by side look flat.

Slightly different petal color adds dimension.

This outline can be part of the design on the petal squares that you use, or they can just be in the imagination of the viewer. If you use the design lines of a floral print to create your outline, remember that the printed lines do not have to match exactly. Also, lines do not have to match within the flower. When viewed from a distance, the eye blurs and blends the outline and interior, filling in any imperfections. Outline quilting around blossoms adds dimension and further defines their edges.

Sorting by Visual Texture

In *Watercolor Quilts* we suggest that you sort your fabric squares by value. After you have mastered value sorting, it is helpful to further sort the groupings. Place similarly textured fabric squares next to each other. Sort your squares into groups of smoothies, chunkies, reachies, freckles, and petals. Sort the chunkies into subgroups of small-, medium-, and large-scale squares. Sort the freckle fabrics by background value. Sort petal squares by background value and by the colors of the individual petals.

Chunky fabrics at top. Smooth fabrics at bottom.

Reachy fabrics

Petal fabrics with light back- grounds

Sorted by value and texture

Petal fabrics with dark backgrounds

Freckle fabrics

CREATIVE EXPRESSION— YOU CAN DO IT

Most of us long to express ourselves creatively. There is no single way to be, or to become, an artist. Ideas, special moments, or a particular mood or feeling can be expressed in many ways. The artists whose quilts are pictured in this book have chosen to interpret their inspirations using fabric. They have experienced the freedom of finding an idea, exploring it, and expressing themselves.

The process of creatively expressing or interpreting an idea often seems overwhelming. Actually, exercising creative expression is similar to playing a musical instrument, such as the piano. Education and hours of practice are required to play the piano. It takes a commitment to learning techniques and working on exercises, scales, and arpeggios. The more you practice and use your skills, the more confidence you gain. Knowledge builds on experience. Every time you learn a more difficult composition, you take risks. As you make mistakes, you practice to correct them. Learning to interpret a composer's ideas is part of the process as well. Sometimes for fun or for a challenge, you may try your own ideas to make the music sound different. Who knows, as you "noodle around" on the piano one evening, you might even compose a piece of your own.

Fabric samples in this section are from the Watercolor Inspirations line, which Pat and Donna developed with South Sea Imports.

So it is with creativity in the visual arts. Creative expression is an ongoing process to cultivate and nurture. To stretch and grow, you must expand your horizons. Try techniques that you have never used before. Consider new and unusual color schemes that take you away from your usual palette. Study themes and variations of themes that push your quiltmaking to the next level.

Practice. Try new solutions. If you make mistakes, learn from them. Or better yet, try to turn the "mistake" into a design success. Be flexible. Give yourself freedom to explore a variety of ideas and to build a repertoire of experiences. Take risks. Remember, one idea often leads to another and another.

Focus on what you like. Give yourself permission to be creative in ways that please *you* instead of trying to please others. Do not judge your work too harshly. Think of the creative process as something you do, while at the same time something that happens to you. You feel freer and come to understand yourself better. You may experience emotions of joy (and sometimes frustration), but all the while you make new discoveries. The results are outward and visible signs of the inner creative process.

Myths About Creativity

"I'm not a creative person."

Too often we associate creativity with the word talent, and we see both of these attributes as divine favors or inherited gifts that make certain people better than others. The truth is, creativity and talent must be used in combination with other qualities, such as perseverance, commitment, education, discipline, and dedication.

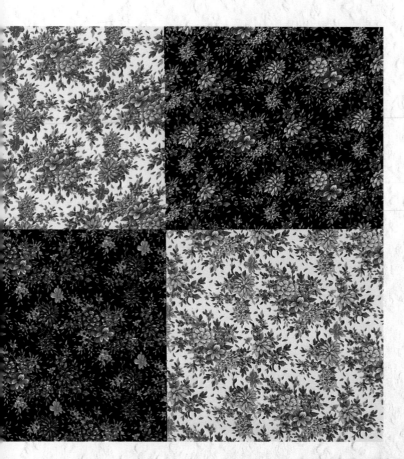

For many of us, creativity has been dormant for a long time. It lives within each of us, like an unopened present. Why not untie the ribbons and remove the wrapping? Give yourself the gift of rediscovering and renewing your creativity. As you allow yourself to be more creative in your daily life, you will find it easier to be creative with your quilting endeavors. Think about it—when you dress in an attractive outfit, plan a pleasing menu for a party, or arrange the pictures on the living room wall, you are being creative.

"I never have a sudden flash of insight or creativity."

Another preconceived notion is that creativity occurs in an instant with a single moment of perception. In fact, there seems to be an ongoing inner process that nurtures creativity. Reflection and contemplation are part of the process. Just as there are rests in music, we need to have moments of stillness and quiet for ourselves. They are just as important as periods of activity. It takes time for ideas to percolate. Sometimes our minds are full of ideas that sift, swirl, and blend. Usually, flashes of insight are small, setting off sparks of creativity that give us a push forward. Once our imaginations are turned on, we try new ideas. One idea often leads to another. Consider all the images, ideas, impressions, and color combinations that fill your mind. Don't toss any of them out yet. Give yourself time to consider them all and to refine the ones you like the best. Eventually, the moment comes when you are ready to put your ideas on paper or to follow your instincts and start working with fabric.

Analyze when and where you are most creative and productive. What environment stimulates you? What time of day do the ideas flow most freely? Does classical music help? Maybe your best ideas strike when you first awake, as with Donna. Perhaps a brisk run with the dog rejuvenates those tired and oxygen-deprived brain cells, as Pat has found works best for her. Maybe you find that you have flashes of brilliance during a relaxing shower, as Pat does (it's too bad graph paper is not waterproof). The point is, create an environment that stimulates and nurtures your creativity.

"I can't get my ideas to work."

It is easy to feel defeated when creative efforts do not turn out as planned or when the process is not going well. Don't give up. Remember that mistakes and discoveries are sometimes linked. Be flexible. Try some "what ifs" and experiment with several different solutions to a problem. Don't ignore that inner voice that asks, What would happen if I try

this? . . . or that? If your efforts don't accomplish what you want, at least you've clarified what doesn't work. If you can't identify the problem easily, try different paths to reach your goal. Sometimes the final product bears little resemblance to the original idea. At other times, a design seems to have a mind and will of its own, so you may as well follow where it leads.

Try being spontaneous. Watch for little flashes of insight that make the light bulb go on over your head. When the creative process, chemistry, and luck are in harmony, and ideas flow, the pieces of the puzzle come together, and you can't seem to do anything wrong. You are in "The Zone." Take delight in the freedom and amazing joy of these moments.

"My creativity is stifled."

As children, we experienced the freedom of art as play. We enjoyed expressing our creativity in many ways, including drawing, painting, singing, and dancing. Creating was easy then because we were impulsive and generally had no constraints. Also, competitiveness was minimal. As we grew older, many of us lost the joy we felt when we did something creative. We felt compelled to do things that turned out "right," in order to meet some external standard. We were disappointed and discouraged when our efforts didn't measure up, and we feared judgmental remarks, including self-criticism.

Perhaps well-meaning adults told us to stop playing around, which suppressed our ideas, and encouraged us to spend our time productively. When we became adults, creative playfulness was buried deep inside.

Expectations, real or imagined, are not conducive to creative expression. Try changing your perception. We tend to think in terms of good or bad, right or wrong. Instead, try telling yourself "my effort is different, not bad." Foster your creativity by being open to new experiences and growth. Learn to make projects that please you, instead of pursuing a direction that others perceive as the "right way."

"The ideas and inspiration are not there."

It is interesting that when the creative juices are flowing, we become completely absorbed in what we are doing. At times like those, nothing can stifle creativity. Meals are forgotten, irons are left on, and the dogs beg for attention.

Like writers and musicians, visual artists sometimes experience "creative blocks." When you find yourself bogged down in the middle of a project, or find that you have stared, for too long, at an empty design wall or blank piece of paper, waiting for inspiration to strike, stop! Analyze the situation. Are external conditions causing distractions and a loss of concentration? Are you tired, or experiencing a lot of stress? Have you criticized

yourself too much or set unrealistic goals? Try some relaxation exercises or words of self-affirmation, which often help. Or take a break. Go for a walk or call some friends, and invite them out to a movie or a bite to eat.

When a project stumps you, approach it from a different direction. For example, tell yourself that "this project is not hard, it is just going to take longer than I thought." Or decide, "I'm going to experiment with various options, mull them over, and make a decision later."

"I may not get it right the first time" is a good attitude to adopt. The quiltmaking process should be fun and playful, not hard work. Creativity cannot be rushed. Just because it doesn't happen today doesn't mean it won't happen tomorrow.

"Making a watercolor quilt is something I could never do."

Yes, you can! Many of the quilts in this book are the maker's second or third watercolor quilt. Many of the pieces shown in *Watercolor Quilts* were the maker's first watercolor quilt. The most essential ingredient is an adequate stash of 2" squares, sorted so you can find what you want when you need it! Practice this affirmation: "Making a watercolor quilt is something I am going to do!" Then *do it!*

Sources of Inspiration

Exposure to a variety of stimuli brings heightened awareness and increased perceptions. Pictures and ideas are stored in the mind, which kindle design inspirations later.

First, observe the magnificence of your surroundings. Act like a sponge. Soak up images, impressions, and sounds. Expand your power to see, feel, and imagine by learning to use all five senses to their fullest—sight, sound, taste, touch, and smell—to capture moments in time.

Our work is influenced by our love of the outdoors, animals, flowers, and especially nature's color combinations and special effects. Watch a calico kitten playing in falling snow. Observe the colors, highlights, shadows, and values. Listen to snow scrunch as you walk through it. Feel the difference in texture between a kitten's soft fur and a handful of snow. Just for fun, catch a falling snowflake on your tongue or lie down and make a snow angel. Savor the depth of encounters such as these, and from that you'll derive a broader base of experience to express through your art.

We both love music, which inspires us in various ways. For example, through listening, singing, or playing an instrument, we "see" and "feel" inspiration, as well as "hear" it. We read books on art, gardening, nature, and interior design. We study photographs and listen to poetry. We clip out pretty or interesting color schemes and pictures from magazines and newspapers and save them for future reference. We buy beautiful and interesting greeting cards and never mail them. We have wonderful gift bags and wrapping paper

we'll never use for their intended purposes, but the designs may someday trigger an idea. Sometimes it seems we have an overabundance of inspirational things, especially when the drawer labeled "Idea Files" won't close.

When choosing a theme or subject to explore, select something that interests you or relates to something you love. When you work with a subject you like, the creative process is more enjoyable, the goal easier to achieve, and the satisfaction greater. When you immerse yourself in an idea and the process of designing and producing a quilt, you are more apt to make an effective, and convincing, artistic statement.

The inspirations for the quilts in this book are as varied and diverse as the artists themselves. Nature, architecture, music, photographs, books, poetry, paintings, posters, memories, moods and feelings, special fabrics, a quilt show theme, geometric shapes, an emotional or moving event, a moment in time, and color schemes for rooms were all sources of inspiration. The makers of these quilts followed their interests and instincts as they worked toward discovery and self-expression. They have communicated not only something about their subject or theme, but something about themselves as well.

Work or Play?

You can take numerous approaches to developing your ideas and visual perceptions. Understanding how you work seems to help the creative process. One way of working will bring out your best creative efforts and seem like play; another work style will frustrate you, making creative expression seem like drudgery.

The following descriptions are brief summaries of just a few ways that people approach design and how they work to bring their design to life. Keep in mind that you may use elements of each design method. Find and use the techniques that allow you to experience the most freedom of expression.

Methodical Approach

If you feel comfortable using pencil and paper and prefer to have a detailed sketch or plan of your project, you approach design methodically. You are likely to have logical thinking skills. You work on an idea for several sessions, planning and finalizing most choices and decisions on paper. Then you begin to work on your design wall, arranging fabric squares.

Pat works this way. "September Spawn" on page 94 was inspired by a trip to Alaska in the summer of 1994. When Pat got home, she went to the library and researched the salmon spawning process. She studied postcards and other artwork depicting the theme. Children's books in particular provided simplified drawings and illustrations of the fish. She first planned her design on graph paper. Pat established where she would develop the dark and light areas of the quilt and where she would place pockets of color. Then she went to her design wall. She placed the salmon first, and then filled in much of the background before realizing that more salmon were needed. A master plan had been established, but she modified the design later.

Intuitive Approach

If you consider detailed design plans a waste of your time, you probably have a more intuitive, spontaneous approach to design. You like to make decisions as you go, possessing a freedom of spirit that allows experimentation in the middle of a project.

Donna is one of these people. When designing "Rhapsody in Bloom" on page 36 in her mind, Donna's first inspiration was her love of music, particularly the piano. For many months she collected visual ideas from music posters, books, magazines, her flower garden, and other sources. One day, a flash of insight moved one idea to the forefront and all the other collected images fell in place. Why not place a grand piano in a garden setting to combine her love of music with her passion for flowers? Donna played with her ideas as she placed the fabric squares on her design wall. After completing the outline of the piano, she filled it in by creating flowers. Then she developed the background and floral areas to give the feeling of a lush garden.

We have noticed that Donna, using the intuitive approach, has to spend more time refining her ideas on the design wall than Pat does when she uses her methodical approach.

Goal-Oriented Approach

Are setting and accomplishing goals high on your list of priorities? Goal-oriented people find it important to their well-being to finish projects in a timely manner. They like to have a sense of order in their world. Pat used to be one of these people, until she started working with Donna!

Process-Oriented Approach

Do you enjoy the process of designing and making the quilt as much as finishing it? Can you leave a project unfinished without carrying around bucket-loads of guilt? If your answer to both of these questions is yes, then you tend to be a process-oriented person, like Donna.

All of us have similarities and differences in our working styles. You need to be flexible while working on emerging designs. Sometimes a project wants to do its own thing, and you may need to make adjustments as you work. There is no right or wrong way to design and create a watercolor quilt. Just relax and let ideas flow and designs develop!

Planning a Specific Design

How does one plan a specific design? Some people have an intuitive sense of what they want to accomplish and do not work well with structured design principles. Others need guidance and support to make their ideas become reality. We offer the following information for your consideration. If you have a preferred approach, you have the freedom to step out on your own and disregard this material any time you wish. Or you may decide to use all of the suggested steps, but in a different order.

Our first rule is that it is okay to break the rules. The object of the design process is to please yourself and communicate what you want to say. You may work with paper and pencil, or you may go directly to your design wall and begin working with your fabrics.

Step One—Design Shape

Decide the overall shape of your design. Do you want it to be square, rectangular (oriented vertically or horizontally), or another shape?

Step Two—Style

Select a style to interpret your idea. You will notice a variety of quilt styles in this book. Some designs based on an image are faithful to the composition of the original. Others loosely interpret a subject or theme. Some are representational and depict an object in a recognizable manner. Others are abstract, emphasizing color and line in a nonrepresentational form.

Still other quilts capture subjects, scenes, and figures with realism. The symbolic style uses representational imagery or color to communicate ideas.

Think about your subject and envision it in various styles. Mix styles. There is no right or wrong here. Try sketching your idea, expressing it in different ways.

Step Three—Composition

As you plan your design, you need to be practical about how much visual information you can include. The charm and beauty of most watercolor quilts is their simplicity. This means that your design need not be an exact replica of your inspiration or idea, but an interpretation that conveys the idea or mood. You may have to eliminate some parts of the design and simplify others. Concentrate more on shadows, highlights, and pockets of color rather than detail. Use this method of "emphasized simplification" to create a strong design.

Consider the spatial relationship between your focused subject (positive space) and the background (negative space). Is there too much of one and not enough of the other?

Put movement in your design. To accomplish this, use curves or an undulating arrangement. For example, balance the contrasts of light and dark values, smooth and coarse textures, and cool and warm colors.

Anchor the bottom of the design. Use darker colors and chunkier textures here to add weight. This is the way we see things in nature. Imagine standing in your flower garden. The flowers in the beds at your feet have distinct details. You can see each leaf, and the earth around them is dark. Now look across the meadow to your neighbor's yard and to the yard beyond that. Individual blossoms and colors moosh together. Colors appear lighter, and you see none of the individual details of flowers, leaves, and grass.

Select a focus and keep the design simple. Do not try to put everything in one quilt.

Where Do I Go from Here?

The quiltmakers whose works appear in this book have experienced satisfaction and a sense of accomplishment by creating something that was pleasing to them. They discovered things along the way, and they share a bit about themselves with us. We look at their quilts and are in awe of their ability to make something so beautiful. Meanwhile, they look at their quilts and see things they would change or do differently next time. We all learn from our projects and our mistakes.

The creative process does not stop here. The more ideas we develop, the more frequent and better our ideas become. We have not reached a plateau; the top is still out of sight. There are many watercolor quilts out there yet to be made. Have lots of fun while you plan and make them!

GALLERY

Rhapsody in Bloom by Donna Ingram Slusser, assisted by Lloyd Slusser, 1995, Pullman, Washington, 52" x 57". Donna combined her love of music and flowers, creating a floral interpretation of a musical theme.

As a child, I spent many hours practicing the piano. It forms the basis of my love of music that flows through every day of my life. Thank you, Mom and Dad, for the opportunity and gift you gave me. Gardening, both vegetable and floral, keeps me in touch with nature's beauty as I observe wondrous changes and momentous happenings. It seemed natural to combine my two loves in this quilt. The quilt's name is a play on words taken from the title of one of my favorite piano concertos.

Water Lilies Through the Mist by Connie Darbellay, 1994, Calgary, Alberta, Canada, 15" x 50". This screen displays the combined artistic efforts of the Darbellay family. The hand-dyed fabric side panels complement the beauty of the watercolor quilt in the center. (Photo by Don Bartolome for Communications Associates, Calgary, Alberta, Canada)

My daughter is a textile major at art college and my husband enjoys furniture construction, so it seemed natural for the three of us to combine our talents and create a screen. I constructed the quilted center panel first so that my daughter could dye coordinating fabric for the two side panels.

Ruby Mountain Autumn by Ellen Krieger, 1994, Pullman, Washington, 34" x 36½". Ellen will always be able to keep the memories of a special trip alive with this landscape.

A trip to the Ruby Mountains in Nevada made a great impression on me. I was overwhelmed by the beauty of the area, and I saw quilt possibilities everywhere. After all, the mountainsides were natural patchwork. When my inspiration is based on nature, I usually take photographs. I use the photographs only to remind me of details. When I begin working, the design takes its own shape and reflects overall impressions and feelings rather than becoming a realistic representation.

Monet: Tulip Fields at Sassenheim by Marlene Kissler, 1994, Seattle, Washington, 67" x 51". For her first art quilt, Marlene beautifully interpreted Monet's landscape in fabric.

I had mulled over the idea of creating a pictorial quilt using the colors and pattern lines of fabrics, instead of seams or appliqué, to create an image. When I saw a picture of Monet's painting, it inspired me to test my idea.

I look for images with colors and shapes that interest the eye. Then I look for fabrics that have the same color combinations and shading necessary to produce the image, using ³/₄" finished squares.

Going Home by Drew Donnelly Benage, 1994, St. Louis, Missouri, 30" x 30". Drew took the watercolor technique in a new direction by combining a batik panel with small squares. The result is a beautiful tropical landscape.

When I first saw the Javanese batik panel, I imagined a colourwash landscape around it. I extended the water and mountains beyond the panel, and used the wrong side of many fabric squares to complete the peach-colored sky. I have been involved in needle arts, clothing design, dressmaking, and tailoring since designing doll clothes as a child. I turned to quiltmaking in the late 1970s, and it has become my primary focus and passion.

Tundra Swan by Ree Nancarrow, 1993, Denali Park, Alaska, 32½" x 34". The Alaskan swan is realistically portrayed in this scene. Appliqué and hand-stitched French knots help to achieve the beauty of this magnificent bird.

It was fun to use an RJR Java handmade batik art panel in this project. I usually design a quilt and then use techniques that most appropriately and effectively convey what I want to say.

Colorwash Module # I by Drew Donnelly Benage, 1993, St. Louis, Missouri, 15" x 20".
Beautiful pockets of color soften this geometric design.

I have enjoyed the geometric designs of Deirdre Amsden for years and used a module from Shirley Liby's "Colorwash Workbook" for this exercise. Although my creative inspiration comes from many sources, I am most often prompted by the fabrics themselves. When I look at fabric, I immediately see a particular style or mood. Selecting and arranging fabric and color are my favorite parts of the quiltmaking process, so watercolor designs are my cup of tea.

Homage to Deirdre Amsden by Lorraine Torrence, 1994, Seattle, Washington, 79" x 55". Rich color combinations add interest to this geometric design.

I start my watercolor quilts with pencil drawings in which I shade areas to create an abstract composition. During the years of making these quilts my style has changed. I have moved toward working with intense color concentrations in different areas rather than using a muted, overall combination colorwash as I did at first.

Leaves Don't Fall. They Descend by Carmen A. Bubar, 1994, Denali Park, Alaska, 48" x 62". Carmen took the title for her quilt from a poem she heard ten years ago in an adult education class. The poem comes to mind every fall as the leaves begin to change color.

My image of fall leaves was easily represented using watercolor-quilt techniques. At the top of the quilt are the shadows you see as you look into a tree full of leaves. In contrast, the sunlight backlights the leaves as they "come winging."

Spring 20½" x 18¾"

Summer 20" x 17½"

Autumn 20¼" x 19"

Winter 19" x 19"

Vivaldi's Four Seasons by Susan I. Jones, 1994, Bellevue, Washington. Susan interpreted the music of Vivaldi beautifully. She quilted these pieces with metallic threads and bound them with lamé.

One of my personal quiltmaking goals is to work in a series to explore a technique or an idea more completely. I also like to listen to classical music when designing and constructing a quilt. I was enjoying Vivaldi's music when I discovered a nearly complete "Spring" on my design board. Evidently, I work intuitively. Completing the series did not take much more discipline or conscious thought, except for emphasis on color and the quilting stitches. Spring has tight blossoms and buds in clear, strong colors. Summer's blooms are more open, slightly faded, and larger. Autumn's bounty and fire-colored foliage reflect the darkening of the season. Winter is all icy and cold colors, overlaid with silvery icicle stitching.

My Rainbow Revisited by Lorraine Ashmore Campbell, 1995, Orange, California, 25" x 37". Two sections intertwine to create this three-dimensional quilt.

My idea for this design seemed to be a simple one, but it required concentration. My creative process usually starts with a need or problem. Then I move to the fabrics that I have on hand. Next, I wonder how far I can stretch the rules. Finally, I worry if my creation will be good enough.

Motion by Marilyn Kay Bower, 1994, Seward, Nebraska, 38" x 38". Marilyn's design focuses on curves. She selected many fabric squares individually and often specially cut them to create the effect of movement.

As a realist landscape painter, it is fun to kick aside the boundaries of natural shapes and colors and experiment with abstract forms and pure colors. I approached this quilt in the same way I begin my paintings, starting with a series of experimental value sketches. Then I chose one sketch and transferred it to graph paper. As the design began to take shape on the flannel board, it started to "talk" to me. I made changes that then, of course, affected all the other parts. This required redoing sections I had previously completed. It's a creative process that is the same whether the medium is paint or fabric.

Wear a Pink Ribbon by Elizabeth Purser Hendricks, 1995, Seattle, Washington, 41" x 50". Elizabeth transferred family photos to fabric and applied silk organza overlays, thereby softening the images and making an effective personal statement.

Breast cancer haunts the women on both sides of my family. This quilt evolved while I worked on it. The original background image of a soft, floral breast seemed so well suited to the watercolor style. The images are of four generations of women in my family, several of whom have had breast cancer. Since my mother died of breast cancer and leukemia twelve years ago, it was particularly difficult, as well as touching, for me to include her image. The writing in the quilting helps tell the story.

Water Lilies by Joan McDonough, 1994, Omaha, Nebraska, 36" x 36". Inspired by a Monet painting, Joan's design reflects the same Impressionistic style.

I enjoyed every step of the quiltmaking process, from choosing the fabrics to quilting by hand. Working with color and the images of the water lilies in the pond was rewarding.

Like a Watered Garden by Terry Waldren, 1994, Anaheim Hills, California. 26" x 26". Shaded borders around a center motif add depth and richness to this engaging design.

Almost as important to me as inspiration is my fabric collection. I don't own one piece of fabric that I wasn't completely in love with at the time I bought it. Fabrics contain so many colors, movements, and subtleties that I lose track of time when I study the interplay of one fabric with another and another and another.

I work best when I have "millions of ideas," so I feed my eyes and my mind with as much information as I can. I have never been at a loss for an idea. I'm just chronically short of time to use them all.

My creative process is one of extending and bending what I see. Creativity is based on curiosity, wondering "why" and "what if." While making watercolor quilts, I wonder if I can make flowers out of patterns that are completely different from one another. The curiosity in making flowers comes from really studying an autumn leaf and seeing greens, reds, and yellows melting into one another and thinking, Could I make something like that too?

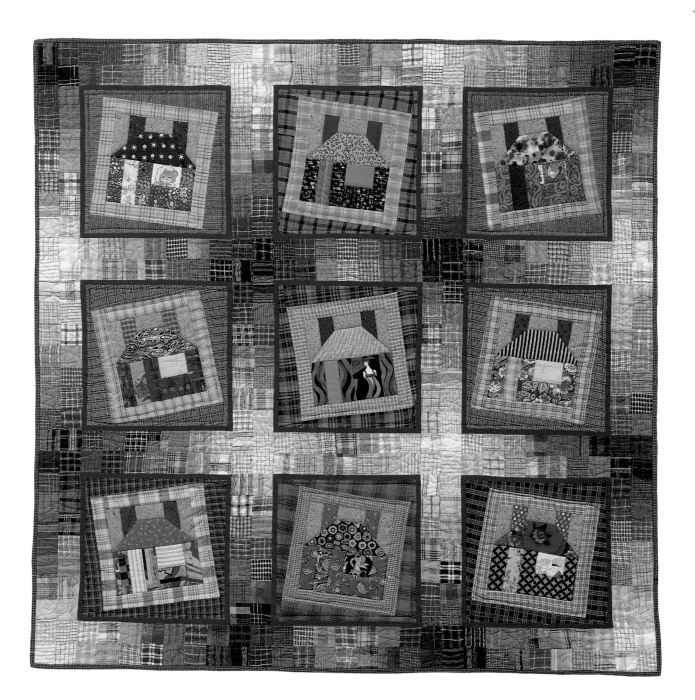

Northwest Movement by Karla Harris, 1995, Hope, Idaho, 43" x 43". Quilted by Wynona Harris King. A graded wash background that effectively uses only plaids sets the mood for this folk-art design.

Influenced by folk-art quilt artist and teacher Mary Lou Wiedman, I had made many house blocks. I had no idea how to set them together in order to complete the project. The idea of combining my house blocks with plaids, which I have collected for some time, seemed perfect. I love watercolor quilts because the style seems to enhance so many designs.

Flower Garden by Ree Nancarrow, Denali Park, Alaska, and Karla Harris, Hope, Idaho, 1993, 53½" x 20½". Quilted by Wynona Harris King. Ree and Karla placed pieced flower blocks, which Ree had won in a quilt shop–sponsored block exchange, on a lovely washed background.

We get together several times a year to work on joint projects. We brainstorm our way through the normal problems encountered when working through an idea. We work at least twelve hours a day, nonstop, since our time together is limited. We work either at Karla's home in Idaho or at Ree's in Alaska. Karla's daughter quilted this project, making it truly a family affair.

Toklat Wolf Pack by Ree Nancarrow, Denali Park, Alaska, and Karla Harris, Hope, Idaho, 1994, 101" x 66". Quilted by Wynona Harris King. Combining representational pieced blocks with a watercolor background effectively portrays this theme from nature.

With only a short time to work together, we roughed out the wolf block and vegetation areas with fabrics. We went to our respective homes—Ree to Alaska and Karla to northern Idaho—to make blocks. Two months later, we got together to figure out how to put the blocks together. Our original intent did not include the use of watercolor techniques; it just evolved as the most effective way to make our statement.

Sailing at Sunset by Cheri Farizel, 1994, Basalt, Colorado, 26" x 31". Cheri made a quilted landscape with a wonderful palette of fabrics. It depicts Reudi Reservoir, which is a high mountain lake outside Basalt, Colorado.

The summer before I began this project, my husband and I bought our first sailboat. I found myself looking more closely at nature while boating, noticing where the water is darkest, how the mountains look from the water, and the different colors that occur in a sunset. I always have a watercolor quilt in progress and take great pleasure in working on one design a little bit at a time. Looking for new fabrics to bring home and talking about the progress with my family is as enjoyable as seeking the perfect 2" square in a piece of fabric.

Jewel of the Mist: A Lighthouse by J. J. Scheri, 1995, Eugene, Oregon, 52" x 29". J. J.'s love of lighthouses is reflected in this seascape, which is a compilation of pictures as well as scenes from her travels.

Lighthouses have always intrigued me. They symbolize many positive values, such as security, guidance, and dedication to the safety of others. I find that I make my best creations when I take the "back burner approach." I let ideas simmer at the back of my mind without letting my intellectual side take over and think too hard about it. I hang the design where I will see it often during the day. Occasionally, I'll stop and gaze for a few moments. Eventually, the creative process simmers long enough, and then I know what to do.

At Water's Edge by Michele Hartley, 1995, Enumclaw, Washington, 24¼" x 21½". Quilted by Cheryl Greenstreet Swain. Michele was inspired by the peace and tranquillity she felt when standing at the water's edge, surrounded by beautiful wildflowers. A particular place of inspiration is Lake Mowich, in Washington state.

This quilt started with a feeling I had. I loosely outlined my areas of color, and then just let it flow.

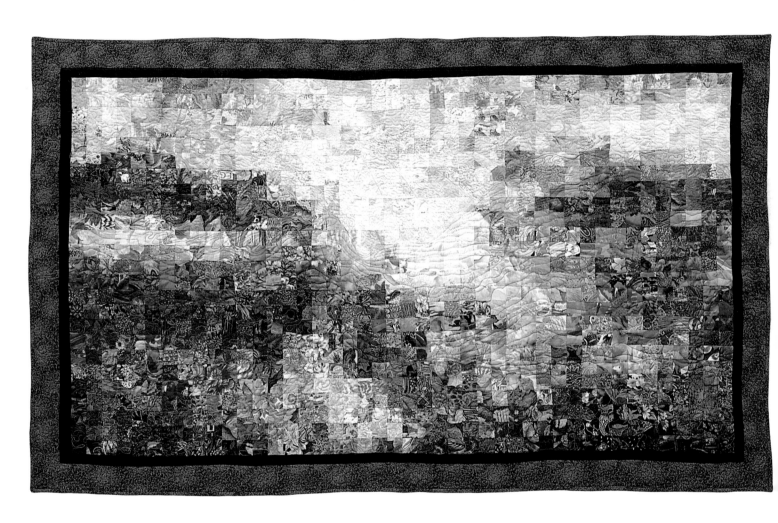

CISter's Sunrise by Marge Davis, 1994, LaVista, Nebraska, 72" x 45". Marge had long wanted a view of an ocean landscape to remind her of what she saw on her honeymoon in Northern California. This attractive Impressionistic seascape is the result.

As I worked on this quilt, I thought about all the friends I have made on the Quilting Forum through CompuServe Information Service. Among other things, we trade fabric. For this quilt, I decided to include the fabrics from each person with whom I had traded during the past few months. This made it a true memory quilt. When I mentioned on the forum that I was making this quilt, I started receiving fabric in the mail nearly every day, along with words of encouragement from all the other CISters (our name for each other). My quilt includes fabric from England, Australia, Germany, Canada, Poland, Italy, France, the Czech Republic, Japan, Singapore, Bali, South Korea, the Virgin Islands, and nearly every state in the United States.

Baskets Aglow by Darlene Harper, 1995, Kennard, Nebraska, 36" x 42". Placing traditional quilt blocks in a watercolor setting produces a delightful effect.

I was working on a challenge project for which I needed to make five blocks. I passed the blocks to the next quilter, who set them together. I decided to make five identical blocks for myself, just to see how I would arrange them. I happened to be in a quilt shop when the owner returned from International Quilt Market in Houston. Her enthusiasm about a watercolor quilts exhibit she had seen there was contagious. She shared her copy of "Watercolor Quilts" with me, and I was inspired to use my five blocks in a watercolor setting.

Four Seasons by Nancy J. Dudley, 1994, Wilsonville, Oregon, 54" x 54". Nancy used the watercolor technique of shading and combining floral fabrics within the traditional Star blocks as well as in the background.

I prefer to work with a design on graph paper and shade the drawing with values of gray. I then go to my fabric stash and choose a group of fabrics to use in the quilt. I need flexibility for watercolor quilts, because the addition of one fabric may set up a color change for a large part of the design. When working on watercolor quilts, I just go with the flow.

Diamantine by Shirley Perryman, 1995, Cary, North Carolina, 53" x 54½". This design is a composite of many Oriental rugs that Shirley saw while looking for furnishings for her new house.

I am in the process of moving, and it has been a challenge to work in less than ideal conditions—in a small, dark apartment, with an improvised design wall and fabric in packing boxes. Despite the inconveniences, I am encouraged that nothing can stifle my creativity. For this project, I was forced to make a graphed sketch ahead of time and stick to it. The quilt flowed together rather easily with all that planning. Looking back, I was frustrated that I could not just dive right in and work with fabric, but not having to undo any of my work was the payoff.

Color Conspiracy by Jennifer Christeck, Mission Viejo, California, and Barbara Jennings, Lake Forest, California, 1994, 48" x 48". Jennifer and Barbara are employees of Hoffman California Fabrics. Although making quilts is not in their official job descriptions, for the past three years Hoffman has asked them to make quilts for each trade show season.

Although we each have distinct styles, working together encourages a sense of experimentation and commitment.

This quilt is our first watercolor attempt. Naturally, we made the entire quilt with Hoffman fabrics. Our challenge to ourselves was to use only fabrics that had been relegated to the scrap bin. Several times each day we dug through the pile in the sample department, retrieving anything that might make a 2" finished square. Our fellow workers laughed at us, until they saw what we were doing with all those little bitty scraps. It was great fun.

Uncle John's Pond by Marca Davies, 1994, Port Townsend, Washington, 40" x 48". Marca created pond and garden quilts by combining watercolor techniques with ideas from author-teachers Judy Warren and Joan Colvin.

We raised koi (carp), which were bothered by heron and raccoons. We finally had to give the koi to some people who did not have these animal problems. I made the heron quilt for my husband, John, to be "his pond."

Garden Gate by Marca Davies, 1994, Port Townsend, Washington, 40" x 48". This quilt is the companion piece to "Uncle John's Pond" on the facing page.

Passioné de Monet by Avis B. Caddell, 1994, Victoria, British Columbia, Canada, 53½" x 41½". Avis placed five elegant fans on a neutral background and surrounded them with a graded wash border.

After I made my first couple of colourwash pieces I found that I wanted to colourwash nearly everything! I also wanted to branch out from 2" squares. For this quilt, I placed the completed fans on my design wall and moved them around until I liked their positions. To help with this process, I cut out some paper fans to scale and arranged them on graph paper. For the most part, I completed the neutral background with ninepatches, with additional squares placed here and there to fill in.

Victorian Fancy by Avis B. Caddell, 1995, Victoria, British Columbia, Canada, 51" x 76".
Avis developed the idea for this quilt as she worked on her first fan quilt, "Passioné de Monet," on the facing page.

My challenge in making this second fan quilt was threefold. First, I wanted to create more movement than in the first fan quilt. Second, I wanted to experiment with variations of the original fans. And finally, I wanted to explore silk painting and use it in a quilt, so I painted the silk that was used to create the flowing ribbon.

On the Beach by Sharon Heslop Wiser, 1995, Pullman, Washington, 36" x 30". This seascape highlights a love of travel and bird watching shared by Sharon and her husband.

A dramatic sunset on a beach in California was the main source of inspiration for this project. On another beach in Oregon, I fell in love with the Oyster Catchers with their pink legs and red bills. I tried to capture, in fabric, the glow of the sun and the reflection of the sky on a wet beach. The subtle look I wanted to achieve was elusive and I had to use the wrong side of brighter and darker squares to yield the muted coloring and desired texture.

I enjoy the soft blending I can obtain with small squares of fabric. Sometimes it is when the colors blend, and sometimes it is the designs printed on the fabrics that make the pieces come together.

Sunrise Surprise by Bernice Molmen, 1995, Salem, Oregon, 41½" x 41½". Influenced by a heron design workshop taught by Joan Colvin, author of *Quilts from Nature*, Bee decided to create a watercolor background for these birds.

This quilt received its name because the project came about so unexpectedly. I just happened to have all the right fabrics for the birds and the background in my stash. Hence the surprise. I am an enthusiastic quilter who loves to try new things, and watercolor quilts have proved to be an exciting and joyous challenge.

My View of the World by Laura Heine, 1991, Billings, Montana, 43" x 55". Color, texture, and light all play an important role in Laura's quilts.

This quilt was inspired by a Camille Pissarro painting, "Women in a Field." Although the quilt is very different from the actual painting, the houses in the quilt resemble the houses in the background of the painting. I added the lattice window as an afterthought, because the quilt didn't seem to have the depth I was trying to achieve. The lattice in the windows made it work.

A Rose is a Rose is a Rose by Laura Heine, 1990, Billings, Montana, 70" x 80½". Many of Laura's quilts have a floral touch, which is apparent in her use of multiple images of roses.

I very much love flowers. My garden is a great inspiration in the summer. Nature seems to provide a huge source of healing and strength in my life.

La Puerta Azul (The Blue Door) by Joli Springer, 1994, Carbondale, Colorado, 37" x 37". Joli found a piece of decorator fabric and used it to make the courtyard tree that arches over the blue door.

This quilt was inspired by my love of Southwestern architecture. My husband built our stucco home two years ago. It was during our information-gathering phase that I learned the color blue is often used to frame windows and doors of adobe homes and is thought to prevent evil spirits from entering the dwelling.

I am guided, during my creative process, by my need to communicate with whoever will see my work or receive it as a gift. I want to create in order to share and evoke thoughts. The watercolor quilt process has become my path to a re-emergence of my creative nature. It has been curative, and I am newly energized by the bond between quilters and their work.

Copper Pot Impression by Joli Springer, 1994, Carbondale, Colorado, 38" x 57". The copper-colored border defines the pot and lends an overall Asian flavor to the quilt.

Originally my watercolor quilts were abstract in nature. This was my first attempt at something pictorial. It just emerged on the design wall. I enjoyed creating the pot first; the copper-colored squares seemed particularly warm. The stems and blossom areas developed easily, and after adding the copper metallic border, I was inspired to quilt the pot portion with copper metallic thread. The quilting process was a perfect outlet for my creative energy. I have long admired the art of watercolor painting because of the fluid movement and soft images.

Summer Garden by Elise Miiller, 1994, Calgary, Alberta, Canada, 46" x 36". Elise's inspiration for this idyllic scene came from photographs of gardens she found in magazines, cards, and other sources.

I wanted to do a challenging project. I sought fabrics that would convey the image of the garden I had in my mind, a garden that would invite the viewer to enter. Outside the gate, one can only glimpse the colors, beauty, and peace the garden offers those who wander through. Watercolor quilts have provided me with an opportunity to combine my love of form and color with my love of fabric.

Spring After the Ice Storm (It Did Come) by Sylvia Gentry Richardson, 1994, Marion, Virginia, 45" x 66".
Memories of picket fences and flower-filled baskets prompted this tribute to spring.

In February 1994 we had a devastating ice storm in the East. It hit our mountain area the hardest. It left whole forests without treetops, blocked roads, damaged houses, and caused electricity to be off for days. We all wondered if there was anything left to bloom, but spring did come in all its glory! I began this project with an image in my mind, a bare design board, and many fabric squares. I let the fabrics do the "talking." I enjoyed this "painterly" project.

Summer Wreath by Ruby Stolz, 1994, Carbondale, Colorado, 43" x 51". Forty years of quilting, combined with her painting background, attracted Ruby to the watercolor process. Combining many little squares is similar to blending paints.

I started to design a flower arrangement using the Hogarth curve, but it soon became evident that the fabric pieces were taking over, and a wreath began to emerge. Finding fabrics for the fade-out areas proved to be a challenge, and I soon discovered that the reverse sides of the fabrics added a wonderful new dimension.

True Love by Connie James, 1994, Kent, Washington, 33½" x 35". This quilt is a romantic floral interpretation of two overlapping hearts, which Connie made to commemorate thirty-nine years of marriage.

I just wait for an idea to hit; then I go to work. I usually concentrate more on the value of the print than the color. But this piece seemed to flow better when I worked with color in mind.

I have given away many of my quilts. I designed and made this quilt after my husband asked me to make something for the two of us.

Colorwash Basket by Pat Linder, 1994, Kila, Montana, 74" x 76". Pockets of color serve as a backdrop for this lovely basket bursting with flowers. Collection of In The Beginning quilt shop, Seattle, Washington.

This was an all-consuming project. I dreamed about it. I couldn't wait to begin working on it every day. I bought and begged fabrics that contained just the right colors. I began with a value sketch because I didn't have any idea where the colors would lead. I find that some quilts, like this one, seem to make themselves—they just flow.

Well-Urned Respite by Doreen Cronkite Burbank, 1994, Windham, New Hampshire, 58½" x 64". A large number of floral fabrics with black backgrounds inspired Doreen to design the urn. The outer edge of the bouquet is an excellent example of the usefulness of "reachy" fabrics.

I was in the midst of working on quilts for my own book, using 5" charm squares, when I was given "Watercolor Quilts." I was so intrigued by the watercolor idea that I put my projects on hold for a week while I assembled this quilt top. Hence the name.

Because I was already working with 5" squares, I just cut them into fourths, making 2" finished squares instead of the 1½" finished squares the authors recommended. The project turned out to be somewhat larger than was practical, so the smaller squares would have been better. I drew the urn on graph paper, and from there the project just "grew" into this floral arrangement. It was great fun, and my respite was indeed "well-urned."

Sally's Tree by Helen Matthews, 1994, Eugene, Oregon, 42" x 30". Helen's first watercolor quilt expresses her love of nature in all its beauty. Collection of Sally Weston.

This was my first attempt at a watercolor quilt, which I made as a surprise gift on the occasion of a good friend's birthday. We live among the trees in Oregon, so this watercolor depiction of a tree seemed appropriate. I have found enormous freedom in thinking and planning watercolor quilts.

I am an Australian who has lived in the United States for many years. I exchange ideas and fabrics with my sister, Lessa Siegele, who lives in Australia. Some of our exchanged fabrics found their way into this quilt. The viewer will find small Australian animals, flowers, and gum nuts tucked among the branches.

Mama Will Fix It by Karen Spriggs Bridges, 1994, Springfield, Oregon, 46" x 46". Karen named this quilt for her mother, who helped make it possible for her to take a watercolor class. Also, as the mother of four children, Karen herself is always fixing something that has been broken.

I have painted for many years, using a variety of media, but I have always had a deep love for sewing and fabric. The French Impressionists have long been my favorite painters, so the transition from painting to quilting was natural.

A Tear for Laura by Maurine Roy, 1993, Edmonds, Washington, 42" x 52". Through the years, quiltmaking has provided a means of expressing emotion. Maurine used her creative energy to find solace while making this memorial quilt.

"A Tear for Laura" is what I call my "therapy quilt" for my little granddaughter, Laura Michelle Gunderson, who was stillborn on October 25, 1993. I started working without any definite idea. As I placed the squares on my work wall, the design gradually started taking form. As my quilt progressed, my pain began to ease. Somehow, working with all those tiny pieces of fabric helped me to resolve my feelings.

I think the most difficult part of making a watercolor quilt is knowing when to stop. You just have to say, "that's it," for there will always be one more square to replace, one more to turn over, and one more way to change the effect. Once you step into the world of quilting, you find there are no limitations placed on your creativity or the depth of your feelings.

Baptism by Anna Assink, 1994, Yakima, Washington, 28" x 23". Anna's use of trapunto and fourteen colors of metallic thread highlights the dove in this reverent design. Collection of Philip Assink.

My ninety-year-old mother's renewed interest in quilting four years ago was the impetus behind my passion to work in this art form.

I started my design by placing different hues in each corner. As I worked toward the lighter hues in the center, I visualized the dove descending. The design expresses a vision of the beauty of baptism as it relates to my Christian faith. This was a gift to my son, who is a minister.

Alive in Christ by Dianne Schrader Picton, 1994, Scribner, Nebraska. In her role as worship leader, Dianne can wear this beautiful stole that not only has religious significance, but exemplifies a traditional women's art form—quilting.

This was my first quilting project. A friend encouraged me to try a watercolor quilt and furnished the squares. As I worked with the fabrics, the project took on a life of its own. The first night I worked until 2 A.M. I made this stole for the green season of the church year, the Sundays after Pentecost. It expresses changes—growth, blossoming, and yielding fruit—that are part of the Christian's life in Christ.

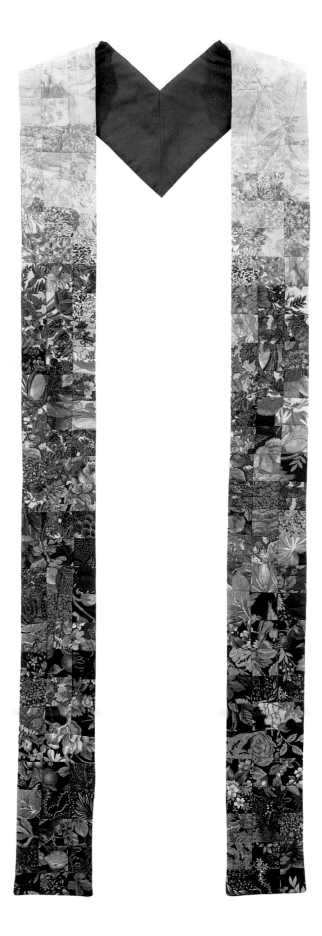

Cathedral on the Rhine by Eleanor Kiser Cole, 1995, Pullman, Washington, 31½" x 42½". Eleanor used broderie perse and appliqué techniques to create a stained-glass window in a lovely garden setting.

During a cruise on the Rhine River, I noticed that every little town seemed to have a cathedral. One cathedral we visited had especially beautiful stained-glass windows. When I decided to do a water-color project, the beautiful stone cathedrals and their stained-glass windows came to mind.

I started quilting when I had grandchildren. I have gone from being just a grandmother to what my husband calls "an addict." He too is involved in quilting now—as a cutter of many 2" squares.

Cosmos Field by Yumiko Hirasawa, 1994, Yokohama, Japan, 64" x 58". Appliqué flowers enhance this beautiful view. Quilts, flowers, and friends can communicate in any language!

I love the cosmos flowers, especially fields of cosmos. I did not have many floral-print fabrics suitable for these blossoms, so I used rose-print fabrics instead. Even though I used gradations of pink fabrics for cosmos, the design looked like a spring landscape filled with pretty, unidentifiable flowers. To make my field of cosmos, I added appliquéd blossoms. My quilting lines represent cosmos waving in a gentle breeze.

Morning Delight by Lloyd Slusser, 1995, Pullman, Washington, 36" x 36". Lloyd was inspired by the watercolor quilts made by his wife, Donna. He put his paints and brushes away, learned how to quilt, and now uses fabrics as his art medium of choice.

For this particular project, I took a photograph of a clump of bamboo growing in our backyard. This is a plant that I'm usually trying to eradicate. This year I just let it grow. In the fall, it developed beautiful colors, and I found them quite inspirational. As I worked on my piece, I could not create with fabric the design and colors in the photograph or in the picture in my mind. I kept reworking the project, and one day I finally let it have its way. The brown areas stayed the same, but soon pockets of color and floral impressions emerged. The source of inspiration looks nothing like the finished quilt! My creativity seems to come from my close ties with nature.

Floating Diamonds by Jean Amsden, 1994, Cambridge, England, 32" x 28". Triangles cut from unique fabrics melt into rich pockets of color. Jean is the mother of Deirdre Amsden, the originator of the colourwash technique.

I was given a box full of tiny triangles by someone who did not know what to do with them. I used white fabric to separate the colored shapes, so that the shapes would appear to float on the surface. I just love patterns, colors, and textiles. I was trained as a scientist but discovered later that I prefer art.

Sometimes I Do Windows by Avis B. Caddell, 1994, Victoria, British Columbia, Canada, 52" x 43". Avis thought about doing a colourwash effect in the windows but decided to "wash" the ledges instead. The design just seemed to beg for all the strips of fabric she had already cut.

I saw Judy Mathieson's samples for her Attic Windows class at Quilting by the Sound (in Port Townsend, Washington) in September 1994 and was inspired to make this piece.

My creative process seems to change constantly, so I remain flexible and just enjoy what happens. Sometimes I do fairly detailed drawings, using layers of tracing paper so that I can alter or add to a design. It also lets me try different shading and color options. For other projects, I work on the design wall from start to finish.

Variations on a Churn Dash by Barbara A. Minton, 1994, Benton City, Washington, 33½" x 33½". Washes of color throughout the quilt highlight and add drama to this traditional block design.

I found this technique to be fun and spontaneous. I thoroughly enjoyed it. This was my first effort, but not my last!

Reflections by Donna Ingram Slusser, 1991, Pullman, Washington, 43" x 43". Donna combined watercolor techniques and a traditional design to give a contemporary feeling to this quilt.

I am intrigued by the idea of taking a traditional block and trying "what ifs" to stretch design and color possibilities. I based this project on the Mrs. Bryan's Choice block. I asked myself, "What if I enlarged the block and switched some of the design elements around? What if I tried a palette of analogous colors?" When the design was nearly complete, the transparency effect became evident. It was a delightful discovery. I used my husband's hand-painted fabrics in this quilt.

Three Stars by Kathleen C. Pappas, 1994, Montrose, California, 35" x 28". Kathleen combined her love of stars with a washed background to make her first watercolor quilt.

My source of inspiration for this project was my son's reaction to seeing the book "Watercolor Quilts." He loves Monet's work and hinted that he would like to have a watercolor quilt. I started with a sketch and added three stars. They represent my son and his fiancée as two stars soon to be united as one. My feelings for them seemed to melt into my work.

Ebb and Flow by Sherri Vaughn, 1995, Mukilteo, Washington, 28" x 28". Sherri wanted to create a piece that had a strong graphic, contemporary quality.

I play with geometric shapes on the computer until I come up with a design I like. I find that I become frustrated while drawing on paper, because ideas come more quickly than I can record them. Working on the computer usually gives me several design choices, and when I can't decide among them, I ask for another opinion. Sometimes I ask another quilter, and sometimes I ask my husband, who has an incredible sense of design.

Flowered Star by Kay Green, 1994, Redmond, Washington, 94" x 94". Quilted by Barbara Troyer, Walnut Creek, Ohio. Kay selected traditional star designs and used watercolor techniques to make them. The blending of the floral fabrics softens the strong lines of the stars.

I based the design on the Union Army Encircled Star Block. I chose a full Lone Star for the center star and made partial Lone Stars for the star points. I wanted the color gradation to change, from dark colors at the center to lighter colors, and then back to dark colors at the outer points. Each side of the pieced border contains a Star block at the center of a chain of Pinwheel blocks. I used strips leftover from making the Lone Star to make the binding.

Changing Views IV by Bonny Tinling, 1995, Vista, California, 93" x 93". Contrasting pockets of warm and cool colors combine to give a luminous effect. Collection of Mary Rose Mueller.

This is one of several works that involves manipulation of formal design elements, such as hue, value, and line. Most often I work from a shaded drawing. Rather than placing colors on paper, I work from colors that are in my head. Colors are subject to change as I go along.

Septimber Spawn by Patricia Maixner Magaret, 1995, Pullman, Washington, 50" x 60".
Quilted by Cheryl Greenstreet Swain. Pat subtly portrays salmon swimming to spawn in
this quilt inspired by a trip to Alaska.

While visiting my son in Alaska in the summer of 1994, I saw, for the first time, salmon as they laboriously returned to their spawning grounds to lay eggs, finally find tranquillity, and then succumb. Observing this simple yet remarkable life process overwhelmed me. I made this quilt as a reminder that we were never promised that life would be easy. But if, like the salmon, we persevere through upstream currents, we will have peace at the end of our journey.

Dream Garden by Patricia Maixner Magaret and Donna Ingram Slusser, 1994, Pullman, Washington, 24" x 28½". A bed of pastel flowers spills into the background and borders of this lovely garden. Collection of Nancy J. Martin.

It was fun for us to combine our creative efforts to make this quilt for Nancy Martin, our publisher. We respect each other's differences and unique styles, which allows us to capitalize on our strengths. The design reflects Nancy's love of floral fabrics and pastel colors.

Enticement—A Little Peek at Heaven by Patricia Maixner Magaret, 1995, Pullman, Washington, 55" x 44".
Inspired by early morning walks, Pat used "petal" and "reachy" fabrics to create a summertime garden.

My life is greatly inspired by nature. Everywhere I look I see little miracles, all gifts from our Father in heaven and his earthly helper, Mother Nature. The Bible says, "For since the creation of the world God's invisible qualities—his eternal power and divine nature—have been clearly seen, being understood from what has been made . . ." (Rom. 1:20)

I see heaven in the flowers in my garden, in the wildlife that scampers to find cover, and in a brilliant, sunlit morning sky. This quilt speaks to all of these.

Tribute to January by Patricia Maixner Magaret, 1995, 46½" x 43½". Quilted by Cheryl Greenstreet Swain. Pat limited this pictorial representation to a palette of black, white, and gray.

I recently discovered that while living in Yosemite National Park as a child, one of my baby-sitters was the daughter of Ansel Adams. I was excited about making a black-and-white watercolor quilt, reminiscent of Adams's photographs. The limited palette resulted in a wintry look. I completed the quilt top on January 8, which happens to be my birthday and that of Elvis Presley. I included Elvis fabric in this design. If you look closely, you might see him resting on one of the mountains.

Late Fall—Ketchikan, Alaska by Marcia Kenoyer, 1994, Ketchikan, Alaska, 31¼" x 40". This quilt is a reflection of the colors and the atmosphere outside Marcia's window.

The idea of painting a picture with fabric really appealed to me. The quilt was "in progress" on my wall for about two months. I spent one or two hours each day moving the pieces around, and the ideas for the quilt floated and stirred in my head all day long. I sometimes started over, working in fits and starts.

Celestory Window by Pat Young, 1994, Laguna Hills, California, 26" x 39". Pat's quilt derives its name from its resemblance to a stained-glass window. A quilted vine grows toward the sky, adding depth and texture.

My original inspiration was a quilt pictured on page 58 of "Watercolor Quilts." My project had a mind of its own, however, and the result is what it wanted to be. As the saying goes, "If you don't have what you want, want what you have." I fell in love with my quilt. I took Polaroid photos during every step of its progress. The photos proved to be invaluable. By studying them, I saw areas within my design that required more attention.

Lions and Tigers and Bears by Kathleen Thomas, 1994, Albuquerque, New Mexico, 36½" x 43". Kathy loves to use novelty fabrics in her watercolor quilts, which explains the title of this piece. Inspiration photo by Putnay Thomas.

The source of inspiration for this project was the beautiful, vast, and colorful sky of New Mexico, which is great for hot-air ballooning. I wanted to create something original and was successful when I finally stopped looking at other ideas and environments and turned my focus toward my immediate surroundings.

I work quickly, putting squares of fabric on my design wall. Then I spend a lot of time reworking the design.

Daddy Lives in the Mountains by Sara Jane Perino, 1995, Pullman, Washington, 48" x 54". Appliqué and watercolor techniques create the feeling of a silhouetted, wintry landscape on a bright, moonlit night.

When starting a quilt, I first visualize the finished project. I include scenes I see in my everyday life in my visualization and sketch them on graph paper.

Several things inspired me to make this quilt. The cold and quiet of winter and the enormous sky you see in the mountains. My son's interest in the moon and my family viewing the moon through his telescope also inspired me. The homey warmth of log cabins came to mind, as did my father, who lives in the Rocky Mountains.

Around the Corner by Cheri Moland, 1994, Veradale, Washington, 30" x 30". Cheri's inspiration for this Impressionistic animal portrait was a black-and-white photograph taken years ago at Yakima Meadows, a horse racetrack in Yakima, Washington.

I like working with photos, taking a moment or a memory that has importance to me, and bringing it back to life with the watercolor process. Black-and-white photos are the most fun because I can fill in colors to create a mood.

I based this quilt on one of many photos taken during fifteen years of working with and training racehorses. I now run a small business that specializes in horse blankets and equipment for the horse-racing industry.

In His Solitude by Judy Abdel-Monem, 1995, Moscow, Idaho, 42" x 41". Judy used a palette of fabrics to make this intriguing interpretation of a painting by Georges Seurat, "Model in Profile."

I design in my head first. Then I'm off to the quilt shop to look at fabrics and figure out what colors I'm going to use. By the time I'm ready to start, I have a pretty good idea how my quilt is going to look, although it doesn't always turn out the way I imagined it. I work with graph paper, and I design by trial and error until I get the look I want. I love animals and I particularly enjoyed incorporating many novelty and safari prints into this quilt.

Just Horsing Around in Sarasota by Maureen Carlson, 1994, Moline, Illinois, 53" x 65". Maureen's graded washes, seahorses, and appliquéd seaweed combine to create this enchanting underwater scene.

I began this project with a sketch, after a visit to the Mote Marine Laboratory in Sarasota, Florida, to study seahorses. Then I moved to my flannel wall. I cut 2" squares from Hoffman batiks, lamé, and my own hand-dyed fabrics. The appliquéd seaweed and border developed as the piece progressed.

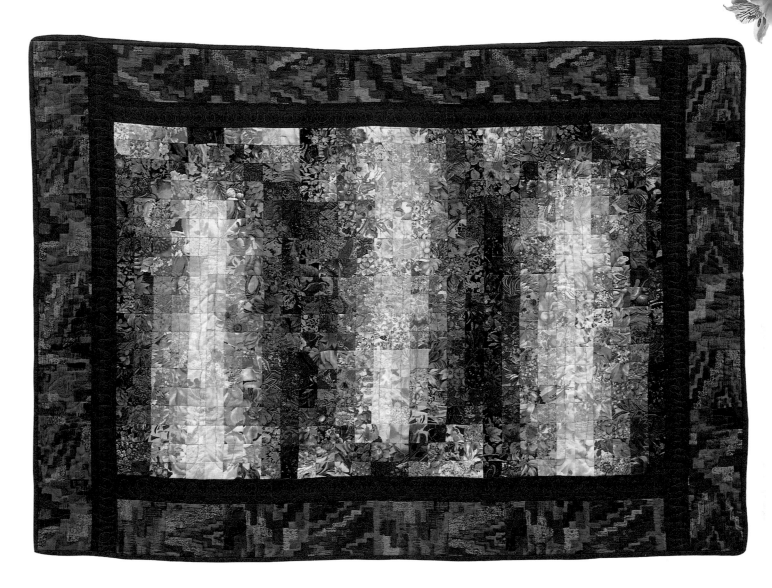

Watercolor Study VII by Cami Smith, 1994, Edmonds, Washington, 58" x 42". Inspired by a design from *Colorwash Workbook* by Shirley Liby, Cami made separate panels, then combined them to complete the quilt.

As a mother of two young children, I often find my creative time in short, interrupted segments. I always have stacks of art, flower, and quilt books around. Studying the pictures is something I can do with my children. I find that watercolor quilts are easy for me to make because once I have the main design on my wall, I can switch small pieces around and still attend to my family.

I Beg Your Pardon . . . I Never Promised You a Rose Garden by Beth Garrison, 1994, Sitka, Alaska, 27½"
x 31½". Beth created pretty floral impressions based on memories of rose gardens and hydrangeas from
the Lake Quinault area of Washington state.

*Watercolor quilts are a strong contrast to my usual style—bold, geometric, reminiscent of Amish
quilts. I like working with small pieces of watercolor fabrics on a vertical surface, much like working
a jigsaw puzzle on a dining-room table. I also enjoy the interplay of color and value. I sometimes
spend hours changing fabric swatches in one area to see what the overall effect might be.*

Picket Fence by Sandy Boyd, 1994, Glenwood Springs, Colorado, 39½" x 31". Sandy's quilt captures emotions and memories in fabric, reaching out to help a community heal from tragedy.

As I walked to work on a particularly beautiful morning last summer, I admired a lovely, old-fashioned flower garden. I was inspired to try to capture this little garden's humble, peaceful prettiness. Soon after, a forest fire threatened Glenwood Springs and fourteen young firefighters lost their lives fighting the fire. Saddened townspeople and business owners wore and displayed purple to honor the firefighters. My quilt is an effort to express the sadness that remained when the calm beauty of our everyday lives returned. Control is only an illusion, despite our efforts to set limits, put up fences, plant beautiful flowers, and make plans. Life is a series of individual events that take on meaning when seen as a whole, as watercolor quilts are collections of separate pieces that only take on shape when seen from a distance.

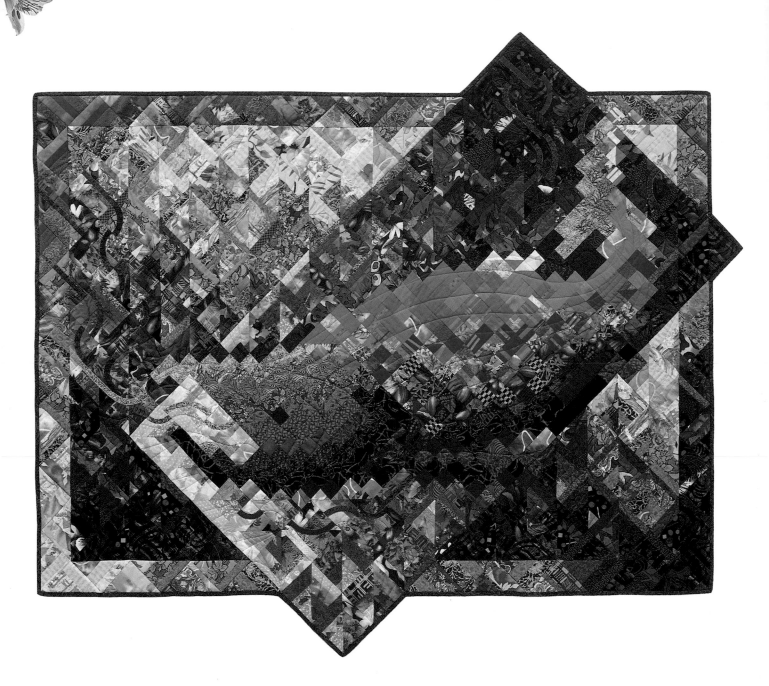

Spawning Red Salmon by Ree Nancarrow, 1993, Denali Park, Alaska, 74" x 64½". Ree's background in art helped her create this stunning piece. The idea of making a red salmon quilt had been stirring in her mind for quite some time.

Watercolor quilts give a sense of depth and space that is unique. Influenced by Margaret Miller's "Strips that Sizzle" technique, I sewed strips together, cut them into triangles, and essentially washed them across the surface of the quilt for the background. I drew the salmon, transferred it to graph paper, and then constructed it of fabric squares containing appropriate colors and prints.

A River Runs Through It by Valerie C. Arcement and Ethel Howey, 1994, San Antonio, Texas, 47½" x 54 ¼". Depicting San Antonio's natural beauty, this original design is an outstanding example of the watercolor technique. It is a symbol of friendship between two sister cities. Owned by the city of Kumamoto, Japan. (Photo by Bibb Gault, Bud Shannon/Photography, Inc., San Antonio, Texas)

Kumamoto, Japan, and San Antonio are sister cities. In October 1993 we traveled to Kumamoto to participate in a quilt display at the City Art Museum. The exhibit included ten quilts made by individual members of the Greater San Antonio Guild. Mrs. Sumiko Maeda, instructor for the Kumamoto quilting group and director of the exhibit, asked us to create a special quilt to hang in the new International Trade Exhibit Hall. Back home, Valerie sketched a design. With the help of several other guild members, we worked many hours during the next four months to complete the quilt. It was presented to the mayor of Kumamoto, Yasumoto Tajiri, during of the center's opening ceremony in September 1994. Members of the Greater San Antonio Quilt Guild who worked on the quilt are: Ethel Howey, Valerie Arcement, Anna Toon, Donna Semmes, Nancy Klaerner, Linda Knieriem, and Jean Powell. It was quilted by Linda Petrey Carlson.

AFTERWORD—
THANKS AND GOOD LUCK!

he watercolor technique has been well received. We thank you and everyone in the quilting community. We have enjoyed many wonderful opportunities—to travel, teach, meet new quilters far and wide, and see sights we never dreamed we would see.

Quilters are a great group of people, whether they live in large urban centers or in rural areas, whether they are beginners or have years of experience. They are all eager to discover and learn. Most of all, they are willing to share themselves, their time, and their talent. We are always inspired by our students. We find their creative enthusiasm contagious and exciting, and we often learn more from them than they do from us.

In this book, there are many beautiful watercolor quilts, and the best are yet to come. Expand your horizons, try watercolor techniques, and create a quilted masterpiece.

Bibliography

Amsden, Deirdre. *Colourwash Quilts*. Bothell, Wash.: That Patchwork Place, Inc., 1994.

Brookes, Mona. *Drawing for Older Children and Teens*. Los Angeles: Jeremy P. Tarcher, Inc., 1991.

Colvin, Joan. *Quilts from Nature*. Bothell, Wash.: That Patchwork Place, Inc., 1993.

Leland, Nita. The *Creative Artist*. Cincinnati, Ohio: North Light Books, 1990.

Magaret, Patricia Maixner and Donna Ingram Slusser. *Watercolor Quilts*. Bothell, Wash.: That Patchwork Place, Inc., 1993.

Warner, Sally. *Encouraging the Artist in Yourself*. New York: St. Martin's Press, 1991.

Warren, Judi. *Fabric Postcards*. Paducah, Ky.: American Quilter's Society, 1994.

Publications and Products

THAT PATCHWORK PLACE TITLES:

AMERICA'S BEST-LOVED QUILT BOOKS®

All New Copy Art for Quilters
All-Star Sampler • Roxanne Carter
Appliquilt® for Christmas • Tonee White
Appliquilt® to Go • Tonee White
Appliquilt® Your ABCs • Tonee White
Around the Block with Judy Hopkins
At Home with Quilts • Nancy J. Martin
Baltimore Bouquets • Mimi Dietrich
Bargello Quilts • Marge Edie
Beyond Charm Quilts
 • Catherine L. McIntee & Tammy L. Porath
Bias Square® Miniatures • Christine Carlson
Blockbender Quilts • Margaret J. Miller
Block by Block • Beth Donaldson
Borders by Design • Paulette Peters
The Border Workbook • Janet Kime
Calicoes & Quilts Unlimited
 • Judy Betts Morrison
The Cat's Meow • Janet Kime
Celebrate! with Little Quilts • Alice Berg,
 Mary Ellen Von Holt & Sylvia Johnson
Celebrating the Quilt
Class-Act Quilts
*Classic Quilts with Precise Foundation
 Piecing* • Tricia Lund & Judy Pollard
Color: The Quilter's Guide • Christine Barnes
Colourwash Quilts • Deirdre Amsden
Crazy but Pieceable • Hollie A. Milne
Crazy Rags • Deborah Brunner
Decorate with Quilts & Collections
 • Nancy J. Martin
Design Your Own Quilts • Judy Hopkins
Down the Rotary Road with Judy Hopkins
Dress Daze • Judy Murrah
Dressed by the Best
The Easy Art of Appliqué
 • Mimi Dietrich & Roxi Eppler
Easy Machine Paper Piecing • Carol Doak
*Easy Mix & Match Machine Paper
 Piecing* • Carol Doak
Easy Paper-Pieced Keepsake Quilts
 • Carol Doak
Easy Reversible Vests • Carol Doak
Easy Seasonal Wall Quilts • Deborah J.
 Moffett-Hall
Easy Star Sampler • Roxanne Carter
A Fine Finish • Cody Mazuran
*Five- and Seven-Patch Blocks & Quilts for
 the ScrapSaver* • Judy Hopkins
*Four-Patch Blocks & Quilts for the
 ScrapSaver* • Judy Hopkins
Freedom in Design • Mia Rozmyn
From a Quilter's Garden • Gabrielle Swain
Go Wild with Quilts • Margaret Rolfe
Go Wild with Quilts—Again! • Margaret Rolfe
Great Expectations • Karey Bresenhan
 with Alice Kish & Gay E. McFarland
Hand-Dyed Fabric Made Easy
 • Adriene Buffington
Happy Endings • Mimi Dietrich
Honoring the Seasons • Takako Onoyama
Jacket Jazz • Judy Murrah

Jacket Jazz Encore • Judy Murrah
The Joy of Quilting
 • Joan Hanson & Mary Hickey
Kids Can Quilt • Barbara J. Eikmeier
Life in the Country with Country Threads
 • Mary Tendall & Connie Tesene
Little Quilts • Alice Berg, Mary Ellen Von Holt &
 Sylvia Johnson
Lively Little Logs • Donna McConnell
Living with Little Quilts • Alice Berg,
 Mary Ellen Von Holt & Sylvia Johnson
The Log Cabin Design Workbook
 • Christal Carter
Lora & Company • Lora Rocke
Loving Stitches • Jeana Kimball
*Machine Needlelace and Other
 Embellishment Techniques* • Judy Simmons
Machine Quilting Made Easy • Maurine Noble
*Magic Base Blocks for Unlimited Quilt
 Designs* • Patty Barney & Cooky Schock
Miniature Baltimore Album Quilts
 • Jenifer Buechel
Mirror Manipulations • Gail Valentine
More Jazz from Judy Murrah
More Quilts for Baby • Ursula Reikes
More Strip-Pieced Watercolor Magic
 • Deanna Spingola
*Nine-Patch Blocks & Quilts for the
 ScrapSaver* • Judy Hopkins
No Big Deal • Deborah L. White
Once upon a Quilt
 • Bonnie Kaster & Virginia Athey
Patchwork Pantry
 • Suzette Halferty & Carol C. Porter
A Perfect Match (revised) • Donna Lynn
 Thomas
A Pioneer Doll and Her Quilts • Mary Hickey
Press for Success • Myrna Giesbrecht
Quilted for Christmas, Book II
Quilted for Christmas, Book III
Quilted for Christmas, Book IV
Quilted Landscapes • Joan Blalock
Quilted Legends of the West
 • Judy Zehner & Kim Mosher
Quilted Sea Tapestries • Ginny Eckley
A Quilter's Ark • Margaret Rolfe
Quilting Design Sourcebook • Dorothy Osler
Quilting Makes the Quilt • Lee Cleland
Quilting Up a Storm • Lydia Quigley
Quilts: An American Legacy • Mimi Dietrich
Quilts for Baby • Ursula Reikes
Quilts for Red-Letter Days • Janet Kime
Quilts from Nature • Joan Colvin
Quilts Say It Best • Eileen Westfall
Refrigerator Art Quilts • Jennifer Paulson
Rotary Riot • Judy Hopkins & Nancy J. Martin
Rotary Roundup
 • Judy Hopkins & Nancy J. Martin
Round Robin Quilts
 • Pat Magaret & Donna Slusser
Sensational Settings • Joan Hanson
Sew a Work of Art Inside and Out
 • Charlotte Bird
*Shortcuts: A Concise Guide to Rotary
 Cutting* • Donna Lynn Thomas
Show Me How to Paper-Piece • Carol Doak
Simply Scrappy Quilts • Nancy J. Martin

Small Talk • Donna Lynn Thomas
Square Dance • Martha Thompson
Start with Squares • Martha Thompson
Strip-Pieced Watercolor Magic
 • Deanna Spingola
Stripples • Donna Lynn Thomas
Stripples Strikes Again! • Donna Lynn Thomas
Strips That Sizzle • Margaret J. Miller
Sunbonnet Sue All Through the Year
 • Sue Linker
Template-Free® Quilts and Borders
 • Trudie Hughes
Threadplay with Libby Lehman • Libby Lehman
Through the Window & Beyond
 • Lynne Edwards
The Total Bedroom • Donna Babylon
Traditional Quilts with Painless Borders
 • Sally Schneider & Barbara J. Eikmeier
Transitions • Andrea Balosky
Tropical Punch • Marilyn Dorwart
True Style • Peggy True
The Ultimate Book of Quilt Labels
 • Margo J. Clabo
Variations in Chenille • Nannette Holmberg
Victorian Elegance • Lezette Thomason
Watercolor Impressions
 • Pat Magaret & Donna Slusser
Watercolor Quilts
 • Pat Magaret & Donna Slusser
Weave It! Quilt It! Wear It!
 • Mary Anne Caplinger
Welcome to the North Pole
 • Piece O' Cake Designs
Whimsies & Whynots • Mary Lou Weidman
WOW! Wool-on-Wool Folk Art Quilts
 • Janet Carija Brandt
Your First Quilt Book (or it should be!)
 • Carol Doak

4", 6", 8" & metric Bias Square® • BiRangle™
Ruby Beholder® • ScrapMaster • Bias Stripper™
Shortcuts to America's Best-Loved Quilts (video)

FIBER STUDIO PRESS TITLES:
The Art of Handmade Paper and
 Collage • Cheryl Stevenson
Complex Cloth • Jane Dunnewold
Dyes & Paints • Elin Noble
*Erika Carter: Personal Imagery in
 Art Quilts* • Erika Carter
*Fine Art Quilts: Work by Artists of the
 Contemporary QuiltArt
 Association*
Inspiration Odyssey • Diana Swim Wessel
The Nature of Design • Joan Colvin
Thread Magic • Ellen Anne Eddy
*Velda Newman: A Painter's Approach
 to Quilt Design* • Velda Newman with
 Christine Barnes

Many titles are available at your local quilt shop.
For more information, write for a free color catalog
to Martingale & Company, PO Box 118, Bothell,
WA 98041-0118 USA.

☎ U.S. and Canada, call **1-800-426-3126** for the
name and location of the quilt shop nearest you.
Int'l: 1-425-483-3313 **Fax:** 1-425-486-7596
E-mail: info@patchwork.com
Web: www.patchwork.com   2.98